LEAVING MY
After the Journey
HOMELAND

My New Home After Somalia

CRABTREE
PUBLISHING COMPANY
WWW.CRABTREEBOOKS.COM

Heather C. Hudak

CRABTREE
PUBLISHING COMPANY
WWW.CRABTREEBOOKS.COM

Author: Heather C. Hudak

Editors: Sarah Eason, Harriet McGregor, and Janine Deschenes

Proofreader and indexer: Wendy Scavuzzo

Editorial director: Kathy Middleton

Design: Paul Myerscough and Jessica Moon

Photo research: Rachel Blount

Production coordinator and Prepress technician: Ken Wright

Print coordinator: Katherine Berti

Consultant: Hawa Sabriye

Written, developed, and produced by Calcium

Publisher's Note: The story presented in this book is a fictional account based on extensive research of real-life accounts by refugees, with the aim of reflecting the true experience of refugee children and their families.

Photo Credits:
t=Top, c=Center, b=Bottom, l= Left, r=Right

Cover: Shutterstock

Inside: Jessica Moon: pp. 5tl, 5bl; Shutterstock: A40757: p. 14b; Alljoh: p. 19; Koldunova Anna: p. 1l; Authentic travel: pp. 12-13; Krien de Jong: p. 26t; Digitalskillet: p. 13b; Dotshock: p. 26b; Elenabsl: p. 21r; Free Wind 2014: pp. 18c, 20r; Great Vector Elements: p. 22bl; Greens87: p. 1bg; Sadik Gulec: pp. 9r, 28b; Hikrcn: pp. 7, 14t, 16r; IsoVector: p. 20b; Iuliia N: p. 23l; Martyn Jandula: p. 15; Helga Khorimarko: pp. 3, 18b; Lawkeeper: p. 23tr; LineTale: p. 23r; LplusD: p. 16b; Macrovector: p. 12b; Roland Magnusson: pp. 10b, 11, 21l, 22br; Oleksiy Mark: p. 25t; MDOGAN: pp. 5r, 9tl; Mspoint: p. 28t; Olyvia: p. 18t; Angela Ostafichuk: p. 25b; Phil Pasquini: p. 27; Photographer RM: p. 22t; Elena Pominova: p. 24; Radiokafka: p. 17; Viktorija Reuta: p. 15r; Rolf_52: p. 29c; Linus Strandholm: pp. 16-17t; Irina Strelnikova: p. 11rSudowoodo: p. 29t; Hamza Sulub: p. 6; Wikimedia Commons: USAID Africa Bureau: p. 10tr.

Library and Archives Canada Cataloguing in Publication

Title: My new home after Somalia / Heather C. Hudak.
Names: Hudak, Heather C., 1975- author.
Series: Leaving my homeland: after the journey.
Description: Series statement: Leaving my homeland: after the journey | Includes index.
Identifiers: Canadiana (print) 20190114967 |
 Canadiana (ebook) 20190114983 |
 ISBN 9780778765035 (softcover) |
 ISBN 9780778764977 (hardcover) |
 ISBN 9781427123770 (HTML)
Subjects: LCSH: Refugees—Somalia—Juvenile literature. | LCSH: Refugees—Sweden—Juvenile literature. | LCSH: Refugee children—Somalia—Juvenile literature. | LCSH: Refugee children—Sweden—Juvenile literature. | LCSH: Refugees—Social conditions—Juvenile literature. | LCSH: Somalia—History—1991—Juvenile literature. | LCSH: Somalia—Social conditions—Juvenile literature.
Classification: LCC HV640.5.S8 H83 2019 |
 DDC j305.23086/914096773—dc23

Library of Congress Cataloging-in-Publication Data

Names: Hudak, Heather C., 1975- author.
Title: My new home after Somalia / Heather C. Hudak.
Description: New York : Crabtree Publishing Company, [2019] | Series: Leaving my homeland: after the journey | Includes index.
Identifiers: LCCN 2019023042 (print) | LCCN 2019023043 (ebook) | ISBN 9780778764977 (hardcover) | ISBN 9780778765035 (paperback) | ISBN 9781427123770 (ebook)
Subjects: LCSH: Refugees--Somalia--Juvenile literature. | Refugees--Sweden--Juvenile literature. | Refugee children--Somalia--Juvenile literature. | Refugee children--Sweden--Juvenile literature.
Classification: LCC HV640.5.S8 H83 2019 (print) | LCC HV640.5.S8 (ebook) | DDC 362.7/7914089935406762--dc23
LC record available at https://lccn.loc.gov/2019023042
LC ebook record available at https://lccn.loc.gov/2019023043

Crabtree Publishing Company

www.crabtreebooks.com   1-800-387-7650

Printed in the U.S.A./082019/CG20190712

Published in Canada
Crabtree Publishing
616 Welland Ave.
St. Catharines, Ontario
L2M 5V6

Published in the United States
Crabtree Publishing
PMB 59051
350 Fifth Avenue, 59th Floor
New York, New York 10118

Published in the United Kingdom
Crabtree Publishing
Maritime House
Basin Road North, Hove
BN41 1WR

Published in Australia
Crabtree Publishing
Unit 3 – 5 Currumbin Court
Capalaba
QLD 4157

What Is in This Book?

Fatuma's Story: My New Home in Sweden

*Hi! My name is Fatuma. I am 14 years old. I live in Stockholm, a big city in Sweden. It is a beautiful country in northern Europe. There are a lot of forests where I like to go hiking. I go to a nice school and have many friends. My life has changed so much. Just two years ago, I was living in the Dadaab **refugee** camp in Kenya, where I was born.*

*My family comes from Mogadishu, Somalia. But I have never been there. My parents fled before I was born, after a **civil war** started between the government and different **clans** of people. Each group wanted control of the country. My parents did not leave right away. They had hoped the war would end quickly. They waited for years, but it did not end.*

In 2018, 320,000 Somalis fled their homes due to fighting across the country.

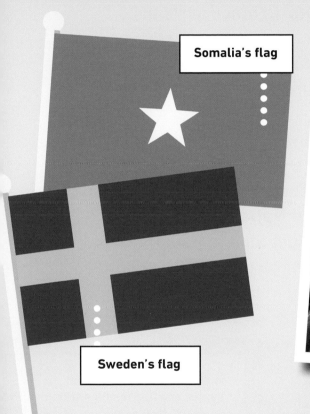

Somalia's flag

Sweden's flag

These refugees live in tents in the Dadaab camp. The United Nations High Commissioner for Refugees (UNHCR) **helps refugees find a** host country.

One day, the store where my father worked was attacked. He was not hurt, but my mother worried he would not be so lucky if there was another attack. That is when they decided to go to Kenya. My older brother, sister, and my ayeeyo (grandmother) went with them. They hoped to find safety in the Dadaab camp until the war was over.

My parents had three more children in Dadaab, including me. Finally, they realized we would not be able to return to Somalia. So they applied to be **resettled** in another country.

My Homeland, Somalia

About 12 million people live in Somalia. It is one of the poorest and least developed countries in the world. Most Somalis live off the land. They grow the food their family needs to survive. In recent times, there have been **droughts**. In other parts of the country, there has been flooding. Farmers cannot feed their families. Hundreds of thousands of people have died. The country is in the midst of a major **humanitarian crisis**.

For decades, there has been a civil war in Somalia. There is no strong government to rule over the entire country. Most people have ties to clans that have fought with each other for control of the country. In the early 1990s, the **United Nations (UN)** and the United States sent peacekeepers to help get food to people. They also tried to restore law and order across the country. They had left by 1995 due to the dangers of working in the area.

Many people have left their homes and fled to cities within Somalia, such as the city of Borama, shown here.

Many homes, hospitals, and schools have been destroyed during the civil war. Somalia does not have enough money to rebuild them.

Today, the civil war continues. Clans and **terrorist** groups, such as al-Shabaab, spread terror. Attacks take place in the streets and many thousands of Somalis have died. More than 3 million Somalis have fled their homes to escape violence and starvation.

The UN asked leaders across Africa to help govern Somalia. Since 2007, about 20,000 African Union peacekeepers have been in Somalia. They fight against al-Shabaab for control of the land. They make sure the government will not be overthrown by the terrorist group. They also teach Somali security forces how to protect the Somali people. In 2017, Mohamed Abdullahi Mohamed was elected president. He promised to help bring peace to Somalia, but he said it would take along time.

Fatuma's Story: Leaving My Homeland

My parents do not talk much about their journey from Somalia to Kenya. My brother and sister were very young. They do not remember the details. I know they all took a bus to Dadaab. The bus was attacked by armed soldiers. The soldiers killed the driver and took everyone's money. My family had to walk the rest of the way. I never met my ayeeyo. She died a few days after they started walking. She could not survive without food and water.

My family had almost nothing when they arrived in Dadaab. The soles of their shoes had holes in them, and their clothes were in tatters. They were starving. It has been 16 years since my family left Mogadishu. But even today, my mother still has nightmares about the journey.

The journey from Mogadishu to Dadaab is 435 miles (700 km).

Ethiopia

Somalia

Mogadishu

Kenya   Dadaab

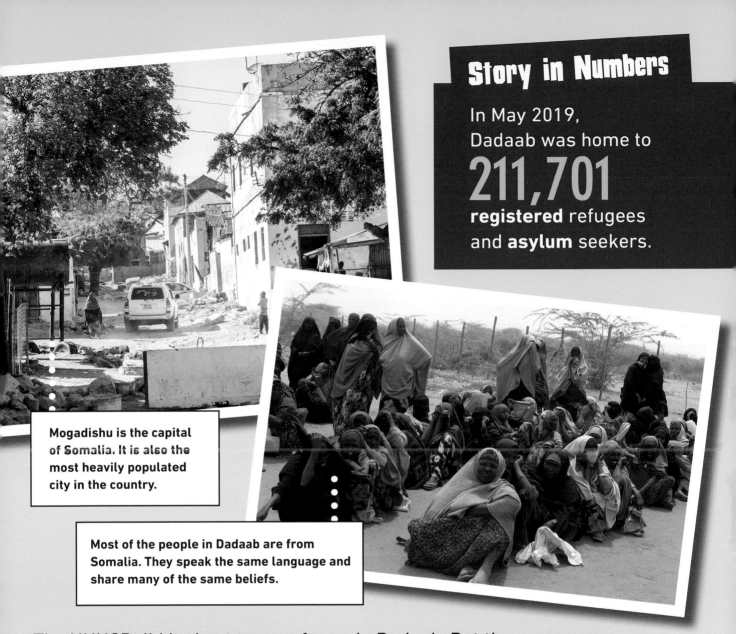

Story in Numbers

In May 2019,
Dadaab was home to

211,701

registered refugees
and **asylum** seekers.

Mogadishu is the capital
of Somalia. It is also the
most heavily populated
city in the country.

Most of the people in Dadaab are from
Somalia. They speak the same language and
share many of the same beliefs.

The UNHCR did its best to care for us in Dadaab. But the camps are overcrowded. They were meant to hold only 90,000 people. At one point, there were nearly 500,000 people living there. New refugees arrived all the time. They told us stories about the attacks in my homeland and how little food there is. It scares me to think about what these poor refugees have lived through. Somalia is my homeland, but I cannot imagine what it would be like to live there.

The Kenyan government wants to close Dadaab because of attacks from al-Shabaab in Kenya. This would force thousands of people to return to Somalia. I hope the government changes its mind. I know there are groups, such as Amnesty International, fighting to keep Dadaab open.

A New Life

Many refugees spend their entire lives in Kenya's refugee camps. The Kenyan government does not allow refugees to leave the camps. This means people cannot find work or build homes. Refugees have no chance to start new lives. Their only hope is for the war in Somalia to end, or to be resettled in a new country. Not all refugees are resettled. Refugees have health tests, security checks, and interviews to find out who has the greatest need. Those with special needs, such as health problems, have the best chance at resettlement.

Sweden tries to make the resettlement process fast and easy. The UNHCR gives the Swedish Migration Agency a list of refugees in need of help. From the list, the agency chooses which refugees to resettle. They get the refugees passports and other documents they need to live in Sweden. The government also makes travel plans for refugees.

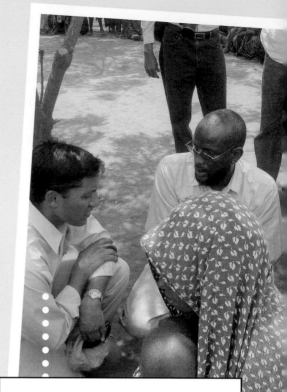

To be considered for resettlement, Somalis must register with the UNHCR. This means they are put on an official list as refugees.

The Swedish Migration Agency prepares refugees for life in Sweden before they leave Kenya. It holds workshops for refugees to learn about life in Sweden.

UN Rights of the Child

The government has a responsibility to make sure your rights are protected. They must help your family protect your rights and create an environment in which you can grow and reach your potential.

Refugees also learn about daily life in Sweden by using the Swedish Migration Agency's websites, videos, and written materials.

Sweden is split into 290 **municipalities**. About 150 municipalities work with the Swedish Migration Agency. Each municipality helps refugees settle into their new homes.

Many other organizations help refugees, too. For example, the Swedish Network of Refugee Support Groups provides advice to refugees. It also helps refugees connect with support groups and services in their communities.

Fatuma's Story: Arriving in Stockholm

I remember how excited we all were to find out we were being resettled. We were chosen because my older sister had been attacked on her way to get water. She escaped with only a few cuts and bruises. But we were afraid it would happen again. Girls face a lot of violence in the Dadaab camp. I have three sisters. The UNHCR knew it was not safe for us there. It took a long time, but finally, we were accepted into Sweden.

I was very afraid to leave the camp. I could not imagine what the world was like outside of it. None of my family knew much about Sweden. People from the Swedish Migration Agency showed us videos and gave us books to read. I felt so much better after I talked to them. Finally, we boarded a bus to the

Jomo Kenyatta International Airport in Nairobi is the largest airport in Kenya. Many refugees travel from there to new homes.

Dearest Asha, I cannot believe we are both in Sweden now. I was so happy to get your e-mail and learn that you have come to Malmo. Saying goodbye to you in the camp was the hardest part. It takes some time to adjust to being in Sweden. I am sure you will have a lot of support from your community. Stockholm is only a few hours away from Malmo by train. Maybe we can meet again soon! Fatuma

airport in Nairobi. It was the first time I had ever left the camp. The agency had someone travel with us all the way to Sweden.

In Sweden, we were met by someone from the municipality of Stockholm. It was both exciting and scary. We did not speak any Swedish. But there was a Somali aid worker named Sauda who helped us. She made plans to meet with us the next day.

Snow covers the ground from December through April in Sweden. This is a big change for Somalis who are used to living in the desert conditions of Dadaab.

Story in Numbers

Sweden accepts about **95 percent** of the refugees referred by the UNHCR. The country takes in about **5,000** refugees each year.

A New Home

Life is hard in Dadaab camp. There are many more people than the camp can hold. Diseases spread quickly, and people have very little privacy. Most refugees live in tents made from sheets of plastic. Others live in small huts called *tukuls*. They are made of grass, twigs, and mud. Insects and animals often get inside the huts.

In Sweden, most homes have separate rooms for eating, living, and sleeping. They are filled with comfortable furniture. Many refugees have never even had their own bedroom, bathroom, or kitchen. Living in a house in Sweden can be a big change for them. Sometimes, it can be hard to get used to this new life. Refugees can take part in programs that help them settle into their lives.

In Dadaab, each refugee is given a space the size of about three bath towels in which to live.

Municipalities set up a place for refugees to live in Sweden. They do this even before the refugee has left Dadaab.

Learning how to get around in a new city can be hard. Most refugees do not speak Swedish when they first arrive. They cannot read signs on buses and streets to know where they are going.

Most refugees cannot afford to pay for their own home when they first arrive. Until they can, they must live in the municipality that accepted them. This is because the municipality gets money from the government to support the refugees who are sent to it. Some refugees have family or friends in a certain part of the country. Sweden tries to settle the refugees nearby. Once they have their own money, refugees can live anywhere in Sweden.

Each municipality helps refugees plan for their future. It helps them get services such as health care. It also gives them a small income for the first two years of their lives in Sweden. The refugees can use the money to pay for basic needs, such as food and clothes.

Fatuma's Story: My New Home

When we got to Stockholm, we were given everything we needed to live there. An apartment had already been set up for us. Sauda took us straight there. She told us that Stockholm has more people than any other municipality in Sweden. It still seemed much less crowded than Dadaab!

The Swedish Migration Agency sent us to Stockholm so we could be near some other members of our family. My aunt, uncle, and cousins were resettled in Sweden more than five years before us. We were so happy to be with them again. Now, we see each other almost every day.

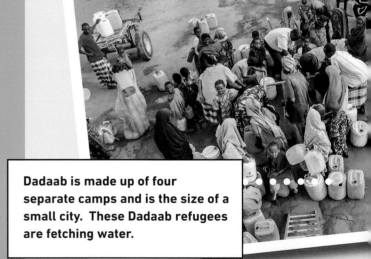

Raggmunk is a popular Swedish food. It is a type of potato pancake fried in butter, served with bacon and berries.

Dadaab is made up of four separate camps and is the size of a small city. These Dadaab refugees are fetching water.

Story in Numbers

Refugees can apply to be Swedish **citizens**

4 to 5 years

after they arrive in the country.

Until we moved to Sweden, I had no idea there were places in the world where food and water were easy to find. There was little food in Dadaab. Here, our cupboards are always full. Raggmunk is one of my favorite foods. In Dadaab, we had to walk to fetch water each day. In Sweden, all we have to do is turn on the tap. I remember the first time I took a hot shower. I had never felt so clean.

People in Stockholm enjoy going out to eat in restaurants. Cinnamon buns and Swedish meatballs are popular foods.

The only thing I owned when I came to Sweden was a small stuffed bear. One of the aid workers gave him to me when I was a little girl. He is ragged and old, but he means a lot to me. My aunt gave me her old cell phone. I have been using it to take pictures of my bear around Stockholm! I have loaded them here, onto our refugee group page. I hope you like them. I am so glad we made the group after we all left the camp. It means we can keep in touch, wherever we are in the world.

A New School

Many schools in Somalia have been destroyed in the civil war. Only 30 percent of children in the country go to school. Even in places where schools have survived the war, most families cannot afford to pay the fees. More boys than girls go to school because girls are often expected to stay home and help the family. Schools do not have enough money to cover their costs or pay teachers. Most children have little education when they arrive at Dadaab.

The United Nations Children's Fund (UNICEF) helps run schools in refugee camps, such as this one in Hargeisa, Somalia.

Story in Numbers

There are
73,394
students in preschool, primary school, and high school in Dadaab.

In Sweden, children go to school for at least 10 years. Each school year lasts from August to June.

Dadaab has a good school system compared with Somalia. There are 22 primary schools and six high schools. There are even learning centers where students can take classes online. There are university programs, too. But the schools are crowded, and few teachers have proper training. There are not enough classrooms, textbooks, and other supplies. Students often drop out early, especially girls. Only a few students complete high school. Most cannot afford to take university classes.

In Sweden, all children are given a very good education. The country has one of the best school systems in the world. Boys and girls are treated as equals. School is free. Children can start pre-school as early as one year of age in Sweden. They attend pre-school until they are six years old. Then they begin regular school and must attend until they are at least 15 years old. Many children in Sweden go to university once they finish high school.

Fatuma's Story: A New Way of Learning

In Dadaab, my parents made sure I went to school every day. Still, it was very different when I got to Sweden. I took a test to see which grade I should be in. Most kids my age were in grade 6. But I was behind in my studies. I was put into grade 5. School in the camp was so different. I learned to do math using rocks. In Sweden, we have calculators.

I started school on the same day as another student from Dadaab, a boy named Aaden. Neither of us spoke Swedish. We met four other students who had come from Dadaab the year before. The school brought in a teacher to help work with us in our language, Somali. This made a big difference. We also took special classes after school to learn Swedish.

Many Muslim girls begin to wear a hijab **when they are about nine years old. They often continue to wear it in their host countries.**

UN Rights of the Child

You have the right to a good quality education. You should be encouraged to go to school to the highest level you can.

Dear ina-adeer (cousin),
I am so glad you finally got high-speed Internet in Dadaab. Now we can write to each other and post on our group page more often. My new school is amazing. The teacher knows so much. She spends a lot of time with each of us. I have my own desk to sit at. There are enough computers and books for everyone. There are even separate bathrooms for the girls so we do not have to share with the boys. I miss you so much! You would love it here. Fatuma

In Sweden, children who cannot walk to school are given free bus passes.

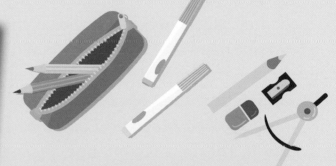

At first, I felt like I did not belong in my new school. I found it hard to make new friends. I could not speak their language. I stood out because of my hijab. Over time, things got better. My cousin Halima helped me with my homework. She practiced Swedish with me. Last year, I joined the handball team at my school. My teacher says I could be very good at the sport if I keep training.

Everything Changes

In recent years, huge numbers of refugees have come to Sweden. This has put a lot of pressure on the country. The country has many programs to help Somali refugees. But these programs are often not enough and need to be improved. Somalis who have spent years living in a camp have special needs compared to other refugees. Many do not have a good education. Others do not have any relevant job skills. Some are nomadic, or move around. In Sweden, they are expected to settle in one place and find steady work. This is a big change.

There is also a lack of housing in Sweden. This means it is getting harder and harder for the government to find places for refugees to live.

More than 45 percent of Somali refugees lived in the countryside in Somalia. It can be difficult for them to get used to life in Swedish towns.

Sweden's Muslim population is growing, and more mosques are being built. Fittja Mosque in Stockholm took nearly 10 years to build and opened in 2007.

UN Rights of the Child

You have the right to practice your own **culture**, language, and religion—or any you choose.

Sweden is a safe country with little crime. Police patrol the streets to help keep people safe.

In Sweden, Somalis often build tight communities among themselves. Their culture is tied to Islam, so most Somalis have beliefs, values, and ways of life that are very different from Swedish culture. As a result, they may find it hard to get used to life in Sweden. This can mean that they miss out on opportunities to build a new life.

Some people in Sweden **discriminate** against Somalis. They think Somalis are a problem for their country. Swedes pay high **taxes**. Some think the money should not be used to support refugees. Somalis are often shown in a negative way on television and in the news, compared with other newcomers to Sweden. Many stories say that Somali refugees are the reason for rising crime across the country. These stories can lead to more **racism**.

Fatuma's Story: My New Way of Life

There were hundreds of thousands of people in Dadaab. Nearly all of them were from Somalia. We all spoke the same language and shared the same beliefs. In Stockholm, I am surrounded by people who are all very different from me. Most are friendly and make me feel welcome. But not everyone is kind.

Somali refugees may experience discrimination even when doing everyday tasks, such as shopping for groceries.

Story in Numbers

There are about

64,000

people living in Sweden who were born in Somalia. Another

30,000

people are Somalis born outside of Somalia.

Soon after we arrived, my father went to buy bread at a bakery. He asked for the price. The woman behind the counter pointed at a sign. My father could not yet read Swedish. When he asked again, the woman told him to go back to his own country where "he belonged." He left the store in shame. This kind of thing happens sometimes. Last week, a man at a bus stop told me to remove my hijab if I wanted to fit in better. I cried myself to sleep that night.

Dear ina-adeer,
I hope you like this video. I wanted to show you what Stockholm looks like at Christmas. This is the Christmas market in the Old Town. It is near the Royal Palace. Each of the red stalls sells food and handicrafts. I remember the first time I came here. I had never seen anything like it. I tried the hot chocolate. It was delicious!

The Christmas market in Stortorget Square is the best-known market in Stockholm.

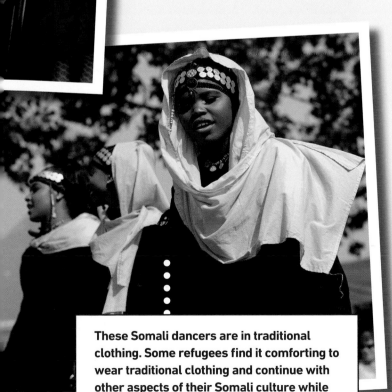

These Somali dancers are in traditional clothing. Some refugees find it comforting to wear traditional clothing and continue with other aspects of their Somali culture while living in their new countries.

My family is trying to get to know the local culture. We visit museums to learn more about Sweden. I wish we had more of a chance to show others our culture. I invited some of the girls on my handball team to my house for dinner. They tried some of the food, but did not finish their plates. I do not think they are used to Somalian food! Still, they are all very nice to me. We go shopping at the mall or to the movies, but I still feel like an outsider at times.

Fatuma's Story: Looking to the Future

Sweden is a beautiful country. The people here love being outdoors. So do I. I like to go hiking with my little sisters. Dadaab was a hot, dry desert. In Stockholm, there are tall trees and green spaces everywhere. I love the smell of freshly cut grass, too.

I have seen how hard it has been for my parents to find work. My mother works as a dishwasher at a small café. My father works in a warehouse at night. That is why I work very hard in school. When I grow up, I want to be an architect so I can design houses that families like mine can afford.

Sweden is known for its natural beauty. The forests around its beautiful lakes, such as Lake Siljan, are perfect for hiking.

College and university are free to all students in Sweden.

Your education should help you use and develop your talents and abilities. It should also help you learn to live peacefully, protect the environment, and respect other people.

Hello Facebook friends in Dadaab! I just saw this story about Ilhan Omar on a news site and wanted to upload it here for you all to read, too. She is the first Somali-born U.S. senator. She grew up in Mogadishu. She fled with her family when the war started, and lived in Dadaab for four years. They were resettled in the United States. She was bullied in school for wearing a hijab, but did not let it bring her down. She worked hard, and it paid off. She gives me hope for the future.

In 2019, Ilhan Omar became one of the U.S. Representatives for Minnesota.

My older brother and sister finished high school when we moved to Sweden, but their grades were not good enough to go to university. Instead, they got jobs in a local store.

I hope to be reunited with my friends who are still in Dadaab, but Swedish laws are changing. It is becoming harder for refugees to come here, and I worry they may never have the chance. Some people here no longer want the government to take in as many refugees. But for now, I am focusing on my hopes for the future—going to university!

Do Not Forget Our Stories!

There is no end in sight to the troubles in Somalia. Al-Shabaab still fights for power. Droughts and floods have left hundreds of thousands of people without homes, food, or other basic needs. Nearly half of the population lives in extreme **poverty**. Returning home is not an option for most Somali refugees.

Refugees who flee Somalia face many dangers on their journey to Dadaab camp. They hope for a better life, but many never leave the camp. When they do get sent to a host country, such as Sweden, they often feel like outsiders.

There are approximately 880,000 Somali refugees around the world, mainly in neighboring countries.

All children have rights, no matter where they live, what their religion is, or whether they are a boy or girl.

A great variety of people live in Stockholm. Many people there make refugees feel welcome.

Sweden provides asylum to more people than any other nation of its size in the developed world. Somalis are one of the largest refugee groups in the country. They have built a strong community in Sweden because they share the same language, culture, and beliefs.

Refugees want a better life. They want to be active in their communities. They want to be treated fairly and with respect. They want to work, contribute to society, and pay taxes. People in host countries can help refugees feel welcome. It is everyone's job to understand their stories and help make a positive change for the future.

Discussion Prompts

1. Why do you think Somali refugees struggle to get used to life in Sweden?
2. Why is it unsafe for Somalis to return to their homeland?
3. How can people help refugees in their host countries?

Glossary

asylum Protection given to refugees by a country

citizens People who belong to a country and have the right to that country's protection

civil war A war between groups of people in the same country

clans Tribes, or groups of people with a shared heritage

culture The shared beliefs, values, customs, traditions, arts, and ways of life of a particular group of people

discriminate To treat someone unfairly because of their race, religion, ethnic group, or other identifiers

droughts Long periods with no rain

hijab Head covering scarf worn by Muslim women in public

host country A country that offers to give refugees a home

humanitarian aid Help given to people in times of great need, such as food and medical care

humanitarian crisis An event that brings harm to the health, safety, and well-being of many people

municipalities Cities or towns with their own local government

poverty The state of being very poor and having few belongings

racism The belief that some races of people are not equal to others

refugee A person who flees from his or her own country to another due to unsafe conditions

registered Officially recorded

resettled Settled in a new or different place

rights Privileges and freedoms protected by law

taxes Money paid to a government for services, such as road maintenance

terrorist A person or group that uses violence to force people to accept a point of view

United Nations (UN) An international organization that promotes peace between countries and helps refugees

United Nations High Commissioner for Refugees (UNHCR) A program that protects and supports refugees everywhere

Learning More

Books

Barghoorn, Linda. *A Refugee's Journey from Somalia* (Leaving My Homeland). Crabtree Publishing Company, 2018.

McPherson, Stephanie Sammartino. *The Global Refugee Crisis: Fleeing Conflict and Violence*. Twenty-First Century Books, 2019.

Ross, Susan. *Kiki and Jacques: A Refugee Story*. Holiday House, 2019.

Ruurs, Margriet. *Stepping Stones: A Refugee Family's Journey*. Orca Book Publishers, 2016.

Websites

www.ducksters.com/geography/country.php?country=Somalia
Learn about the geography and culture of Somalia.

www.cia.gov/library/publications/the-world-factbook/geos/so.html
Learn all about the people, culture, and economy of Somalia.

www.unhcr.org/ke/dadaab-refugee-complex
Find out more about the refugee camp in Dadaab.

www.unicef.org/rightsite/files/uncrcchilldfriendlylanguage.pdf
Learn more about the UN Convention on the Rights of the Child.

Index

About the Author

Heather C. Hudak travels all over the world and loves to learn about different cultures. She has been to more than 50 countries, from Brazil to Indonesia and loads of others in between. When she is not on the road, she enjoys spending time with her husband and many rescue pets.